The Olympic Games

Look for these and other books in the Lucent
Overview series:

Acid Rain
AIDS
Animal Rights
The Beginning of Writing
Cancer
Dealing with Death
Drugs and Sports
Drug Trafficking
Eating Disorders
Endangered Species
Energy Alternatives
Extraterrestrial Life
Garbage
Gun Control
Hazardous Waste
The Holocaust
Homeless Children
Ocean Pollution
Oil Spills
The Olympic Games
Ozone
Population
Rainforests
Smoking
Special Effects in the Movies
Teen Alcoholism
The UFO Challenge
Vietnam

The Olympic Games

by Theodore Knight

LUCENT
B·O·O·K·S

LUCENT *Overview Series*

LUCENT Overview Series

Library of Congress Cataloging-in-Publication Data

Knight, Theodore, 1946-
    The olympic games / by Theodore Knight.
       p.   cm. — (Lucent overview series.)
    Includes bibliographical references and index.
    Summary: An overview of the Olympic Games throughout their history; highlighting some of the achievements, records, and humorous and tragic moments; and discussing such aspects as boycotts, terrorism, and drug use.
    ISBN 1-56006-119-7
    1. Olympics—Juvenile literature.   2. Olympics—History—Juvenile literature. [1. Olympics—History.]   I. Title.   Series.
GV721.5.K56   1991
796.48—dc20   91-15562

© Copyright 1991 by Lucent Books, Inc.
P.O. Box 289011, San Diego, CA 92198-0011

Contents

Introduction

EVERY FOUR YEARS since 1896, athletes from nations all over the world have gathered together in a designated host city for a festival of sports competition called the Olympic Games. Thousands of athletes compete, representing more than 140 nations. As many as five million spectators attend the sixteen days of competition. The Summer Olympics comprise more than twenty sports ranging from archery and basketball, to gymnastics and fencing, to weight lifting and yachting. The Winter Games include a variety of skiing and skating events as well as bobsled and luge competitions. Almost two billion people—or one out of every three people in the world—watch or listen to the Games. With this worldwide audience, the Olympic Games can be described only as a global event.

For all the attention the Olympic Games attract, few people know much about their long history and complex traditions. The ancient Olympic Games began as a major religious festival in ancient Greece. These Games brought the residents of warring city-states together to worship, compete, trade, and negotiate. The modern Olympic Games began at the end of the nineteenth century as an attempt by a single man to create a worldwide festival similar to the ancient Olympics.

(opposite page) Carl Lewis parades with U.S. and Jamaican runners after winning his fourth Olympic gold medal and helping the U.S. relay team set a new world record at the 1984 Los Angeles Olympics.

That man, Baron Pierre de Coubertin, believed that in order to become a successful individual and useful citizen of a modern, progressive nation, a person needed more than a developed intellect. He or she also needed a healthy, developed body and a competitive spirit. De Coubertin was also deeply concerned with finding ways to increase international understanding and goodwill. He created the modern Olympics in hopes of encouraging and increasing individual physical achievement, national progress, and global peace.

When the first modern Olympic Games were held in Athens, Greece, with 311 athletes from ten nations, no one could have imagined that in less than a century, the Games would grow to their present size and significance. Certainly the baron's goal of supporting athletic achievement has been effectively achieved. It is hard for anyone who is not deeply involved in athletics to understand or appreciate the enormous talent and commitment required to even participate in modern Olympic competition. It is difficult also to appreciate how far Olympic athletes have pushed the upper limits of physical achievement.

We now live in a time when boundaries between nations are breaking down and people are becoming increasingly aware of how small this planet is and how interconnected all of its people are. The Olympic Games have played their part in promoting this sense of global unity. The great festival itself provides a unique opportunity for men and women from all over the world to meet and mingle with one another. For a time in the Olympic stadium, competitors and spectators alike put aside their differences and join in the appreciation of supreme individual physical achievement.

If the Olympic Games have played a part in influencing world affairs, then world affairs have changed the Olympics as well. National policies, international disagreements, and even wars have affected the staging of the Games and the decisions and regulations of the Olympic organization. Despite the rising and falling fortunes of the Games, however, they have continued, and it appears they will continue, for a long time to come.

1

The Ancient Olympics

THE OLYMPIC TRADITION began in ancient Greece well over three thousand years ago. It began with religious festivals in which games of skill and contests of strength played an important part. To spectators and competitors alike, these athletic events signified devotion to religious beliefs. An athlete, the Greeks believed, honored the gods by displaying his skill. Those who rigorously and properly performed the religious rituals of the day were rewarded with blessings from the gods. These blessings translated to victory and brought great honor to the athletes, their families, and their cities.

A tradition of religious festivals

These religious festivals were held frequently in ancient Greece. Many large city-states also held a special month-long festival every four years. These festivals were so important to the Greeks that, although the various tribes and city-states fought constantly with one another, during the festival month, all fighting stopped and people were guaranteed safe travel.

Among all the Greek festivals, the largest and most important was the one held in a meadow be-

(opposite page) Ancient Greek athletes competed to honor the gods. This painting depicts a reception for an Olympic victor.

11

side the river Alpheus at the foot of Mount Olympus. This Olympic festival is the historical birthplace of our modern Olympic Games. Mount Olympus was the most sacred site in ancient Greece. Its peak was believed to be the home of the gods. The festival at Olympus was held to honor Zeus, who was the king of the Greek gods, and to celebrate the beginning of human history. According to one of the oldest Greek myths, the human race began as a result of a fight between Zeus and Kronos, the mightiest of the gods. The two wrestled on Olympus for possession of the earth. When Zeus won, he rid the earth of the monsters that inhabited it and then created human beings. For the Greeks, then, the celebrations at Olympus not only honored Zeus as the supreme god, but also celebrated the birth of humanity.

As further honor to their gods, the Greeks built a temple and a huge stadium complex in which to

The original Olympic complex was built at Olympia, Greece to honor the Greek gods.

hold these special Games. The main temple at the Olympic site held a forty-foot-tall statue of Zeus seated on a cedarwood throne decorated with ivory, gold, ebony, and precious stones. The statue's sculptor, known as Phidias, carved Zeus's flesh from ivory, wood, and stone and delicately fashioned a robe and other ornaments from gold. The stadium complex included three major buildings: a stadium designed to hold about fifty thousand spectators; a hippodrome, which contained a long, oval track of about five hundred meters; and a giant gymnasium containing a huge indoor arena, a covered practice running track, hot and cold baths, steam and vapor baths, drying rooms, and rest rooms. Surrounding these structures were many smaller buildings, as well as altars and temples. It appears that following each Olympic festival, statues and altars were added to the site in honor of the newest champions. The elaborate nature of the Olympic site gives us a sense of how important the Olympic festivals were to the Greeks. Only an event of major proportions could have attracted such crowds or justified such elaborate construction for a facility to be used only once every four years.

To the Greeks, Zeus was the supreme creator, and the Olympics were celebrated in his honor.

Legendary beginnings

It is impossible to say precisely when the Olympic festival began. We know that it was very early in Greek history because it is mentioned in some of the writings of the earliest anonymous Greek poets. Several popular Greek legends describe the first Olympic competition. The most popular one tells of a famous chariot race held near Olympus between a king named Œnamaus and a prince named Pelops. Œnamaus, according to legend, had a beautiful daughter named Hippodamia. Œnamaus promised her in marriage to the first man who could find her and then escape in a

Chariot races were one of the first events held in the ancient Olympic stadiums.

chariot with her father in pursuit. Thirteen young men tried and were defeated. Œnamaus put each one to death. Then came Pelops's turn. The race got under way but ended abruptly when the axle on the king's chariot mysteriously broke. Pelops, according to the legend, had cut the axle. The king broke his neck and died. Pelops married Hippodamia and declared himself king. He ordered a great feast day to celebrate his victory and give thanks to Zeus, thus initiating the first Olympic festival.

The earliest written record of the Olympic festival concerns a man named Coroebus. Coroebus apparently won a footrace of about 200 yards (180 meters) at the Olympic festival in 776 B.C. and was rewarded with a wreath of olive branches. Archaeological excavations have uncovered the remains of a temple and other buildings at the Olympic site that date back several centuries before this race. Nevertheless, historians view Coroebus's victory as the start of the ancient

Olympics. From 776 B.C. to A.D. 393, when the Games ended, 293 Olympic festivals were held at Mount Olympus.

Olympic participants

Originally, athletic competition at the Olympic festival was limited to male Greek citizens; foreigners, slaves, and women were barred from competition. Every athlete had to take the Olympic oath, swearing that he had trained for ten months before the Games and that he had done nothing to offend the gods. Athletes who competed in the ancient Olympics were not just average citizens. They had to be wealthy enough to travel to and from the Games and to pay their living expenses while they trained. In the early days of the Games, the only reward was a wreath. Winning athletes, however, were expected to provide huge banquets to celebrate their victories. This meant that competition in the ancient Olympics was mostly for members of the wealthy, ruling class, since only they had enough time and money to take part.

For many centuries, women were barred not only as competitors but also as spectators. The penalty for breaking this rule was death. Even so, some women still tried to watch the Games, even if it meant donning a disguise. One story tells how the mother of a young runner named Pisidorus did just that. When the young man's father died while training him, the mother took over the training and then attended the race disguised as a man. When Pisidorus won the race, the mother's cries of joy were so loud she was discovered. She was not put to death, however. To this day, no one knows why.

As time progressed, Olympic rules changed. By the time of the 128th Olympics, women were allowed to compete in as well as watch the

Throwing the discus was one of the five events in the ancient pentathlon *competition.*

Games. In that year, according to ancient written records, the winner of the chariot race was a woman named Belisiche, from the country of Macedonia, or what is now parts of Greece, Bulgaria, and Yugoslavia.

Earliest events thrill spectators

For many decades (at least up to the time of Coroebus's victory in 776 B.C.) it appears that the festival's athletic competition was confined to a few footraces. As the years passed, more and more races and other athletic events were added, but no records exist to tell us when particular events were added. We do know that footraces, chariot races, wrestling, boxing, and a brutal sport called the *pancratium* were among the early Olympic sports. Pancratium combined boxing, wrestling, biting, kicking, gouging, and strangling. Men were often permanently injured or killed in this event. The *pentathlon*, which combined five sports, was also an early popular event. In the pentathlon, contestants threw a flat wooden and metal plate called a discus and a light spear

The pancratium *was an ancient Olympic contest. It combined boxing, wrestling, kicking, and strangling.*

called a javelin. They also wrestled and competed in the long jump and the sprint.

Records indicate that the wrestling, boxing, and pancratium competitions drew especially huge and enthusiastic crowds. The high level of interest probably stemmed from the strong hostilities between cities and tribes. Because a truce was in effect during the Games, these events offered a chance for athletes from hostile cities to do physical battle with one another. No matter how great their passion for conflict, however, the Greeks' high regard for physical beauty was greater. When it came time to erect statues honoring new Olympic champions, it was the smoothly muscled pentathlon athletes who were honored rather than the bulky wrestlers or the wiry runners.

Chariot races, too, thrilled Olympic spectators. The most important chariot race was the *quadrigae*—a race for light, two-wheeled chariots pulled by four horses. The distance of the race course was twelve laps around two columns at opposite ends of the hippodrome—about ten thousand meters, or six miles. Often as many as forty teams entered the race, and accidents were common on the crowded track. Once, in a race of forty chariots, only one man finished. Everyone else had been injured or killed.

Other ancient events

Three footraces were especially popular. The *dolichos* was a race of twenty-four lengths of the stadium field. The runners ran around two columns, with much shoving and pushing and many injuries. A shorter, similar race, the *diaulos*, was only two stadium lengths. The *stade* was a sprint for one stadium length, or about 883 meters. In addition, foot-soldiers dressed in full armor and carrying their swords and shields ran in a special race.

Footraces were popular events in the original Olympics.

The ancient Olympic Games included pageants and parades along with the athletic competitions.

When the ancient Games were at their peak, they comprised five days of pageants, parades, feasts, and religious rituals as well as the athletic events. Sacrifices were offered daily to all the gods. The athletes themselves offered prayers at the altars of various gods and placed sacrifices and gifts before the statues of previous Olympic victors. City-states tried to outdo each other by presenting the largest and most magnificent sacrifices and gifts. Nothing, however, equaled the spectacle of the third day of the festival when one hundred cattle were ritually slaughtered at once and then burned on a special altar.

Much went on at the Games also that was not

directly connected with either religion or sports. Tribal chiefs, magistrates, kings, and consuls from all over the Greek world used the time of truce at the festival to conduct discussions and to negotiate treaties. Merchants and traders gathered to sell their wares and make trade agreements. Jugglers, musicians, magicians, poets, and fortune-tellers all performed for the crowds.

Olympic decline

The history of the ancient Olympic Games parallels the history of ancient Greece. Over the centuries, as Greece grew to be the most powerful nation in the civilized world, the Olympics grew also in size and importance. When the Roman Empire conquered Greece around 100 B.C., however, Roman culture and beliefs replaced the Greek way of life, and the Olympics went into a decline that lasted for several centuries. For the

After the Romans conquered Greece, the Olympics became a brutal form of entertainment, often including battles between men and animals.

Romans, war and trade were more important than philosophy, religion, or athletics. The Olympic festival lost most of its original significance as a celebration of patriotism and religion. Contestants had once competed to honor the gods and win their blessings; now they wanted to win for themselves. They began to demand prizes and money for competing. With money rather than spiritual rewards at stake, cheating and bribery increased among the athletes and officials. The Games themselves became a brutal form of entertainment. There were battles between animals, battles between men and animals, and combat-to-the-death between gladiators. Real athletic competition faded away. When the Roman emperor Nero built himself a great palace at Olympia and

The Roman emperor Nero gives the "thumbs down," sentencing a gladiator to death.

then entered Olympic events as a competitor, all sense of true competition died. Defeating the emperor was a dangerous thing to do because, as the supreme monarch of the empire, he was considered all-powerful. So Nero was always victorious. Following several centuries as a form of public entertainment that had little to do with the Olympics' religious beginnings, a religious change came to the Roman world. This change ironically signaled the end of the Olympics. In A.D. 393, with the spread of Christianity, the Roman emperor Theodosius I declared an end to all pagan rituals including the Olympics.

In later years, the temples and altars at Olympia were destroyed by invading barbarian tribes. Then, in A.D. 426, Emperor Theodosius II ordered the walls surrounding the Olympic fields completely pulled down. About a century later, several earthquakes completed the ruin of the historical site. The Alpheus River flooded the original Olympic meadow. All signs of the ancient Olympic Games had been completely erased. After well over twelve hundred years, the festival at Olympia had ended. There would be no Olympic Games for more than fifteen hundred years.

The emperor Nero was considered all-powerful, so when he began to enter Olympic events, other competitors were afraid to win. Because Nero was always victorious, the Games became a farce.

2

Revival: The First Modern Olympics

THE MODERN OLYMPIC Games owe their existence to the actions and efforts of one man—Baron Pierre de Coubertin. The baron was born in 1863 into an extremely old and wealthy family of French aristocrats. As a young man, he rejected his family's idle ways and became a social and educational reformer, determined to improve French culture and make it a model for other nations. The baron believed that training a new generation of leaders and workers for a successful, modern society required an educational system that combined intellectual and physical training. He admired the British system of public school education and wrote numerous articles proposing that it be adopted in France. As time passed, he became convinced that his social and educational theories were the answer not just to France's problems but to world conflicts as well.

Growth of an idea

It is not clear exactly when and how Baron de Coubertin's interest in education and sports resulted in the idea for a rebirth of the ancient Olympics. German archaeologists had discovered the site of the ancient Games at Olympia during

(opposite page) A parade of the winners at the first modern Olympic Games, which were held in Athens, Greece in 1896.

six expeditions between 1875 and 1881. Reports of the discoveries gathered a great deal of attention, and de Coubertin read them closely. Here was solid evidence, he believed, of the role physical competition had played in creating the golden civilization of Greece. This was a model for all nations, the baron believed, especially for his native land. Through his efforts, a number of sports federations were founded in France, each devoted to sponsoring and organizing a single sport on a national level. These included fencing, riding, rowing, cycling, boxing, swimming, track, and gymnastics. Then, in 1889, de Coubertin founded the French Sports Union, which tied all of these

Between 1875 and 1881, archaeologists uncovered evidence of the ancient Olympics. The neck of this vase is painted with scenes of footraces and boxing.

individual organizations together.

The baron publicly unveiled his grand Olympic proposal in 1892 at the closing session of the French Sports Union's annual meeting. In his speech, he said that while hopes to completely eliminate war were foolish, hopes to greatly decrease the chances of war were not. "The telegraph, railroads, the telephone, dedicated research congresses and expositions have done more for peace than all the treaties and diplomatic conventions," he told the assembled dignitaries. "Indeed, I expect that athleticism will do even more." He concluded by asking the directors of the sports federations to continue to support the union as they had in the past. He intended, he announced, "to re-establish a great and significant tradition, the Olympic Games."

Baron Pierre de Coubertin founded the modern Olympic Games.

Disappointing response

The baron was profoundly disappointed with the response to his grand, if rather vague, proposal for an international sports festival and competition. No one reacted at all. In the days that followed, when he tried to generate some enthusiasm for the idea, he got blank stares and polite general comments. No one really had any idea what he had in mind. To most people, bringing the ancient Olympic Games back to life was as odd an idea as returning to the worship of Zeus. What, they wondered, was de Coubertin thinking?

The complete lack of response did not stop the baron. He left for the United States in search of support. He visited colleges, universities, and private sports clubs all across the country, talking about his idea to anyone who would listen. Although he was received with respect, no one seemed very excited by the baron's ideas. Undiscouraged, de Coubertin prepared a series of articles for French newspapers and magazines about organized sports in the United States and about university sports programs. In his articles, the baron reiterated that sports and physical competition were an important part of educating the whole person and that athletic competition fostered understanding and cooperation between people.

When he arrived back in Paris, the baron announced plans for an International Athletic Congress to which he invited the leaders of sports organizations from around the world. In June 1894, two thousand delegates representing forty-nine sports in twelve countries gathered at the Sorbonne University in Paris. The congress lasted for a week. Representatives exchanged information about sports in their various countries and discussed the creation of uniform international rules and regulations for particular sports. The last item on the agenda for the last day of the congress was a discussion of the revival of the Olympic Games.

Leaving little to chance

De Coubertin had left little to chance this time. Despite the variety of items on the meeting's agenda, at the opening session the delegates found themselves entering a hall decorated with banners proclaiming that they were attending "The Congress for the Re-establishment of the Olympic Games." The delegates were wined and dined and treated royally throughout the congress, all in an effort to win their hearts and their votes on the subject of the Olympics. The baron later wrote that his intention was "to please and impress" the delegates, that he wanted "not to convince, but to seduce." He used skills as an organizer and promoter to pamper and flatter the delegates. Fabulous luncheons and banquets were set before the members of the delegation. Between

meetings they were treated to exhibitions of gymnastics and other sports. The banquets featured resounding speeches about the great cultural significance of the delegates' work. The evenings concluded with music. For part of one evening's entertainment, the baron commissioned a well-known French composer named Gabriel Fauré to write a choral arrangement based on several ancient Greek poems.

The baron's efforts to arouse enthusiasm in the delegates for the ideals of ancient Greek culture and athleticism paid off. The group voted to hold the new Olympic Games every four years and to locate them in a different city around the world each time. Only amateur athletes, those who received no money for playing, training, or competing, would be allowed to take part. Most important of all—from the baron's point of view—the group voted that the Olympics would be con-

The International Olympic Committee was established to conduct the 1896 Olympics in Athens, Greece.

ducted by an independent International Olympic Committee (IOC) headed by de Coubertin. This impressive international group, cleverly assembled by the baron for just this purpose, had given his idea the powerful endorsement it needed and left all the control and authority in his hands.

Victory and setbacks

Baron de Coubertin had hoped to set the first Olympics six years later in Paris in 1900. The congress was so enthusiastic, however, that it voted to hold the first Games four years earlier, in Athens, Greece, a tribute to the original home of the Olympics. Now that the baron had won his battle, he had little time to savor his victory. An enormous organizational task lay ahead. Planning

The International Olympic Committee chose the site of an ancient stadium in Athens, Greece for the first modern Olympic Games.

for the Athens Games went smoothly for only a short while. The Greek government began to regret its quick acceptance of the honor of hosting the Games. Greece was a poor country, and at the time it was plunging into a deep economic crisis. Also, Greece had practically no modern tradition of sports competition. Most Greek officials had no clear idea exactly what this sports festival they had agreed to was all about. Soon Baron de Coubertin received a letter announcing that Greece was forced to decline the "generous offer" of hosting the Games.

De Coubertin intervenes

The baron immediately sailed to Greece in an effort to change the minds of government officials. He repeatedly visited government offices. He spoke to public and private groups and tirelessly wrote letters to the newspapers. In one letter he observed, "We have a proverb which says that the word *impossible* is not French. Someone told me this morning that the word is Greek, but I didn't believe him." Once again, the baron showed his ability to appeal to people's pride and vanity. Within two weeks, the Olympics was the most popular topic of conversation in Athens. Popular opinion swung in favor of the festival. The government bowed to the pressure and once again agreed to host the Games. It had become a matter of Greek honor that the Games take place in grand style. The government, while unable to offer any direct assistance, authorized a set of commemorative postage stamps honoring the games. Proceeds from sales of the stamps were given to the Olympic Organizing Committee. By February 1895, nearly all of the money needed to finance the Games had been raised.

For the site, the organizers chose the historic ruins of an ancient Greek stadium on the outskirts of Athens, nestled between two hills near the city's dump. In a burst of optimism, the organizers decided to rebuild the stadium to its original splendor using expensive marble. The committee approached a wealthy Greek businessman named George Averoff for a donation to assist in the project. Averoff announced that he would pay not only for rebuilding the stadium but also for the entire festival. Eventually, when all the bills came due, the cost had more than doubled. Averoff paid without complaint. His example encouraged other wealthy Greeks to contribute. With the sudden influx of money, the enthusiastic organizers built tennis courts, swimming pools, a gallery for marksmanship, and a velodrome for cycling events. They decided that, like the ancient Olympics, the first modern Games would be more than an athletic competition. Money was set aside for nightly entertainment—banquets, fireworks, music, and plays. A special budget allowed Athenians to spruce up their city by installing gas lights and re-paving the streets.

Mixed response

While preparations were underway in Athens, Baron de Coubertin set about recruiting competitors and spectators all across Europe. Some countries responded to the idea enthusiastically. The eight-man Hungarian team arrived three weeks early and caused a great stir in Athens as they strutted about in their tight-fitting uniforms. France, the baron's own country, initially did not provide much support. In the end, the French team consisted of two cyclists, some fencers, a runner, and a couple of French tourists who happened to be in Athens at the time. The response from Great Britain was not much better. Athletic officials at Cambridge and Oxford universities showed little interest in the Olympics. The even-

tual British team was only six in number: two official entrants plus an Australian distance runner who was living in London; a British tennis player who happened to be in Athens at the time; and two young employees of the British Embassy in Athens, who entered for the cycling events.

The Americans sent the largest foreign team to Athens. Princeton University allowed four members of its track squad six weeks off from school to travel to Athens. The team captain was from a wealthy Baltimore banking family and paid all the expenses of his teammates. Five members of the Boston Athletic Club and one member of the Suffolk Athletic Club in Massachusetts attended with the help of private donations. One student from Harvard University joined the team, although he was forced to quit the university in or-

George Averoff, a wealthy Greek businessman, funded the construction of this stadium and also financed the entire 1896 Olympics.

der to go. At the last moment, three other Boston men joined the group.

Meanwhile, in Greece, during the year since the first announcement of the Games, sports clubs had sprung up everywhere. In nearly every town and village, young men were hard at work training for Olympic events. Positions on the national team were hotly contested until nearly the opening day of the Games. Greek pride was at stake, as competitors and as hosts.

After fourteen centuries, the rebirth of the Olympics was at hand. On opening day, April 6, 1896, ten nations were represented in Athens by official or unofficial teams: Great Britain, France, Germany, Denmark, Hungary, Switzerland, the United States, Austria, Australia, and Greece. Altogether, there were 311 competitors, with the Greeks making up more than half of the total. The organizers could not have chosen better dates for the Games. April 5, the day before opening day, was Easter Sunday, a day of great feasting and celebration in the Greek Orthodox Church. The opening day of the Games was also the anniversary of Greek national independence. Religious, patriotic, and athletic enthusiasm all mingled together as seventy thousand people crowded into the new Olympic stadium. About fifty thousand more spectators covered the surrounding hillsides with a view into the stadium. As the crowd stood at attention, the Greek king, George I, announced the opening of the First International Games in Athens. And then, without a moment's hesitation, the crowd erupted in whistles, shouts, cheers, and applause.

Revival of the ancient marathon

Of all the events, it was perhaps the marathon that most captured the spirit of the reborn Olympic Games. Nothing like it had been part of the an-

cient Games. But this long-distance footrace, more than any other event, symbolized the determination of the individual human spirit. The marathon also had special meaning to the Greeks, for it honored the epic Athenian victory over the Persians in the battle at Marathon in 496 B.C. Legend has it that an Athenian soldier named Pheidippides ran without stopping the forty kilometers from the battlefield to Athens to deliver the news of victory. "Rejoice, we have won!" he shouted; then he fell dead.

The Olympic marathon race course was to retrace the legendary warrior's own footsteps from Marathon to the stadium in Athens—a distance of about twenty-six miles. Completing the race

Pheidippides ran forty kilometers from Marathon to Athens to tell the city about his army's victory. After he relayed the message, he died. The marathon footrace was started in his remembrance.

would require great stamina and endurance. Thousands of spectators lined the roads of the marathon course and 100,000 more jammed into the stadium to watch the finish. As race time approached, twenty-five runners readied themselves at the starting line. Several coaches on bicycles and a fully equipped, horse-drawn hospital wagon waited nearby. When the gun sounded, Albin Lermusieux of France immediately took the lead and set a fast pace. After fifteen kilometers, Lermusieux was three kilometers ahead of his nearest rivals. An Australian runner named Edwin Flack panicked at the Frenchman's early lead and fought to overtake him. After fighting to the lead twice and then immediately being passed again by Lermusieux, Flack veered off the course and collapsed, unconscious. Soon after, another of the leaders, Arthur Blake of the United States, collapsed with blood running from his shoes. He was carried off to the hospital wagon. Now fatigue was overtaking Lermusieux, and he began to stagger. His coach rode alongside on a bicycle shouting advice. Suddenly, the two men collided and Lermusieux smashed to the ground. Somehow, he got to his feet and staggered on, but he had lost his chance to win.

Spiridon Loues takes the day

Through all this, a wiry, spindly legged Greek runner named Spiridon Loues had been pacing himself behind the leaders. Loues had been one of the very last Greek runners to qualify for the marathon. But from the moment he first heard of the race, Loues had a vision of winning it for the glory of his nation. A peasant from the small village of Marousi, Loues had no sports experience, but his job had given him an ideal opportunity for long-distance training. For years Loues had been a water carrier. Each day he hauled water in containers on the back of his donkey from his native village to a water depot in Athens. Twice each day, he covered the nine-mile route, jogging beside the donkey.

Now, as Loues began passing one fatigued runner after another, he used a devastating psychological ploy. He would very slowly pull past a struggling runner and then allow himself to be passed in turn. Then he would dash past the runner again and pull rapidly ahead. One runner after another dropped out of the race, demoralized by Loues's obvious reserves of stamina and speed. As Loues entered the stadium, the crowd was in a frenzy. Even the dignified king of Greece was so overcome with excitement that he waved his royal hat in the air until the brim tore off. Loues

Spiridon Loues, pictured here on the right, was a Greek water carrier who won the first modern Olympic marathon.

had won for his nation the symbolic victory it
wanted so badly, and he had secured for himself a
permanent place in the hearts of Greek citizens.
As the Greek flag ascended the pole at the top of
the stadium in tribute to the victor and his nation,
thousands in the crowd wept openly with pride.

Triumphant return

When the Athens Games finally drew to a
close ten days after they had begun, the United
States had collected the most gold medals—
eleven to Greece's ten. But the Greeks had accu-
mulated by far the greatest total number of

After the Athens Games, the International Olympic Committee continued planning festivals. Here it is pictured meeting before the 1936 Berlin Olympic Games.

medals, thirty seven, followed by the United States, Germany, France, and Great Britain, in that order. In all the excitement of the Games, and with sufficient victories to satisfy even the most patriotic Greek, it is not hard to understand that the Greeks had come to believe that they were completely responsible for the Olympics. Earlier, Baron de Coubertin had made the politically wise decision to retreat into the background when it became apparent that recruiting athletes from other countries would be difficult for a French-inspired idea. The baron took the occasion of the formal closing dinner of the Games to remind all those assembled that the Olympics were a continuing international event—not a one-time national festival. And he spoke once more of his grand Olympic dream: "We shall not have peace until the prejudices which now separate the different races shall have been outlived," he said. "To attain this end, what better means than to bring the youth of all countries periodically altogether for amicable trials of muscular strength and agility? The Olympic Games, with the ancients, controlled athletics and promoted peace. Is it not visionary to look to them for similar benefactions in the future?"

3

Athletic Achievements

(opposite page) Two weeks prior to competing in the Olympics, Mildred "Babe" Didrikson demonstrated her amazing athletic ability by winning the national team championships as a one-woman team. The second place team had twenty-two members.

THERE IS NO sure formula that can guarantee an athlete a victory in the Olympics. The path to a gold, silver, or bronze medal is different for every competitor. Nevertheless, the history of the modern Olympics shows certain common elements, or combinations of elements, appearing over and over again in the stories of successful Olympians. The chief ingredient, of course, is talent—the gift of better-than-average physical ability. Any athlete who makes it to the Olympics is a great athlete. But a few rise even beyond that point. These are the athletes whose performances on the field seem to have no limits. Sheer talent alone cannot guarantee success, however. Even the most gifted athletes must discipline themselves mentally and physically. They must think like winners and believe they are winners in order to win. And sometimes the will to succeed carries an athlete far beyond his or her natural abilities. Many notable Olympians' medals were the result of spiritual and mental victories rather than just physical prowess. In addition to talent and the will to win, one other element appears over and over again in stories of the achievements of Olympic athletes. That element is innovation, the

Jim Thorpe throws the shot put as part of the decathlon competition at the 1912 Stockholm Olympic Games.

ability to study and understand their particular sport and to improve and refine—perhaps even transform—the skills and techniques it requires.

Blessed with talent

Sometimes an athlete seems so blessed with talent that no one can offer serious competition. In most cases, athletic records creep up by fractions of seconds and last for years without being broken. But occasionally an athlete appears who seems to have leaped a decade or two ahead of everyone else.

The 1912 Stockholm, Sweden, Olympics brought the world's attention to an almost supernaturally gifted athlete. Jim Thorpe, a Sauk and Fox Indian born in the Oklahoma Territory in 1888, made a name for himself while still in college. Thorpe rose quickly as a star in football, basketball, baseball, and track. But it was his performance at the Stockholm Olympics in 1912 that firmly fixed the world's attention on Thorpe. He performed superbly, winning gold medals in the pentathlon and decathlon. Together, these totaled fifteen different events.

In the day-long pentathlon, Thorpe competed in the long jump, discus, javelin, 200-meter and 1500-meter races. He finished first in four of the five events, easily dominating the field of competitors. In the discus, for example, Thorpe's toss sent the lightweight plate flying a full meter (or a little over three feet) farther than the next nearest throw. In the 1500-meter race, where Olympic runners typically finish within tenths of seconds of each other, Thorpe sped to the finish a full five

The mayor of New York pays tribute to Jim Thorpe after Thorpe's stunning performance in the Stockholm Olympics.

seconds ahead of the second-place finisher.

The decathlon, which is a series of ten events, was not scheduled to start for another two days. Instead of taking the day off, Thorpe entered two individual events: the high jump and the long jump. In the high jump athletes propel their bodies over a bar that is raised higher after each successive turn. In the long jump, athletes take a running start and then jump as far as they can into a sand pit. Although Thorpe did not earn a medal in either of these events, he missed third place in the high jump by three-quarters of an inch and finished seventh out of thirty-two competitors in the long jump.

Continuing victories

The decathlon got under way as planned the following day. Usually, competition in the ten events lasts two days. But that year, the unusually large number of entrants forced Olympic officials to spread competition over three days. Thorpe finished first in six of the events and tied with two others for first place in a seventh. He had to settle for second in the last two events. When points were totaled for all ten events, Thorpe had scored another victory. He had set a world record for overall decathlon performance. His performance was so impressive, it would have earned him a silver medal in the decathlon in the 1984 Olympics.

In the 110-meter hurdles, one of the events in which Thorpe finished first, athletes run and leap over ten evenly spaced hurdles, each three feet, six inches in height, without breaking stride. In this race, Olympic runners usually finish a fraction of a second apart. Thorpe astounded spectators by beating the second-place runner by nearly two seconds. Another of the decathlon events is the javelin toss in which an eight-and-a-half-foot-long spear weighing just under two pounds is thrown from a run by the athlete. Thorpe had never thrown a javelin until two months before the Olympics. So it was all the more spectacular when he finished third in a field of twenty-nine in that event. His strong score was just one more example of how fine an all-around athlete he was.

An extraordinary athlete

Thorpe's brand of versatile talent cropped up again in 1932 at the Los Angeles Olympics. Despite the number of records set and the supreme athletic achievements of many competitors, the star of these Games was an eighteen-year-old American track-and-field athlete. Mildred "Babe" Didrikson arrived in Los Angeles just two weeks after a series of stunning victories at the national women's track-and-field championships. During a three-hour competition, she had set world records in the 80-meter hurdles, the javelin, and the high jump. She also won the shot put, the long jump, and the baseball throw, and finished fourth in the discus. When the point totals were announced, Didrikson had won the team title by herself with thirty points. Second place at twenty-two points went to the twenty-two member University of Illinois team.

Despite those victories, Olympic rules in 1932 limited women to competition in three events. Didrikson chose javelin, hurdles, and the high jump. She set world records and took home gold medals in javelin and hurdles and tied a teammate for the world record in the high jump. Didrikson was an aggressive competitor who was determined to succeed. When one method of jumping lacked the momentum she wanted, for example, Didrikson searched for another. She developed an unusual style in the high jump that brought criticism from judges and other jumpers. Traditionally, athletes soared over the high bar feet first.

Mildred Didrikson set a new world record and won a gold medal in the javelin competition at the 1932 Los Angeles Olympic Games.

"Babe" Didrikson sets the world record in the hurdles and wins the gold medal for the event during the 1932 Los Angeles Olympic Games.

Didrikson ignored tradition when she found that she could clear the bar even more efficiently by going over it head first. This innovation cost her a gold medal in the high jump in 1932 but was later adopted by nearly all high jumpers. Two years after the Olympics, Didrikson took up golf and became the best woman professional in the game. In 1950, sportswriters across the country voted her the best female athlete of the first half of the century.

Reaching for records

Athletic excellence was also the trademark of a West German swimmer named Michael Gross. At the 1984 Olympics in Los Angeles, Gross stood out—figuratively and literally. At 6 feet, 7½ inches, Gross stood out in any crowd. His incredibly long

After the 1932 Olympics, Didrikson held the world records in hurdles, high jump, and javelin.

arms covered a "wingspread" of 7 feet, 4³/₄ inches, earning him the nickname "The Albatross" (for the huge seabird with the long wingspan). Gross carried away two world records and four medals from Los Angeles—more than any other male swimmer that year. He won his first gold medal in the 200-meter freestyle race.

In that race, swimmers are free to choose their stroke. In most cases, they use the crawl because it is considered the fastest stroke. Gross's crawl overwhelmed several very strong opponents. In a race that usually is decided by tenths or even hundredths of a second, Gross won by two seconds and two full body lengths. The next day, Gross was scheduled to swim in the 100-meter butterfly.

Michael Gross dives into the pool at the beginning of the men's 100-meter butterfly competition during the 1984 Los Angeles Olympic Games.

Michael Gross waves to the crowd after winning a silver medal in the 200-meter butterfly competition. He also won a gold medal in the 100-meter butterfly and set a new world record.

The butterfly is an odd-looking stroke in which athletes thrash through the water making huge, simultaneous windmill-like strokes with their arms. When all was said and done, Gross had defeated world champion Pablo Morales of the United States and cut three-tenths of a second off Morales's record. The race was so fast that the top six finishers all set national records.

Achieving perfect scores

Records of various types are often set in the Olympics. But a new kind of record, unusual even by Olympic standards, was set in 1976 by a tiny fourteen-year-old Romanian named Nadia Comaneci. Comaneci had been training as a gymnast since she was six years old. In 1976 in Montreal, her training paid off.

Comaneci made Olympic history at the age of fourteen by earning two perfect scores in team competition on the uneven parallel bars and balance beam and seven other perfect scores in indi-

Nadia Comaneci dismounts from the uneven bars at the 1976 Montreal Games to score the first perfect ten in Olympic history.

Nadia Comaneci performs on the balance beam at the 1976 Montreal Olympics. She scored a perfect ten in the event.

vidual competition. Other athletes had made near-perfect scores, but no one in Olympic history had ever received even one perfect score. Those who saw Comaneci gliding and twisting on the uneven parallels and dipping, turning, and tumbling on the balance beam described her performances as flawless. Observers said Comaneci was absolutely unafraid of dangerous moves and seemed oblivious to the millions of people watching her. These and other performances brought Comaneci a silver medal and three gold medals in Montreal. At the age of fourteen, Comaneci had set a new standard for women's gymnastics. Four years later in Moscow, Comaneci earned another two gold medals, two silver medals, and a bronze.

Whatever his or her innate physical gifts, no athlete reaches the Olympics without an extraordinary measure of discipline, both physical and mental. No matter how much talent and physical prowess anyone has, the human body is a delicate instrument. Any small malfunction—a sore muscle, a bruise, a pinched nerve—can cause the body

Wilma Rudolph sets an Olympic record for the women's 200-meter dash at the 1960 Rome Olympics.

to break down. The stride that covered six feet suddenly covers five feet, ten inches. Forty swimming strokes per minute become thirty-six. In the Olympics, every inch, every stroke, counts because this is competition between the very best athletes. Even the very best spend many hours training their bodies and minds to make that extra effort that sets them apart from the others. Some have had to travel great distances to reach that place. This is especially true of a remarkable number of medal winners who had to overcome enormous obstacles to even arrive at the Olympics.

Beating the odds

One such athlete was Wilma Rudolph, a runner on the U.S. women's track team. Rudolph won three gold medals at the 1960 Olympic Games in Rome, the first American woman ever to do so. Her first-place finish in the 100-meter dash tied the world's record, and she set an Olympic record in the 200-meter dash. It was her running of the final leg of the 400-meter relay, however, that showed the world the incredible determination that her friends and acquaintances already knew. The 400-meter women's relay was a battle between the German and American teams. Although the Germans took the lead at the start, by the end of the third leg of the race, the Americans had managed to gain a lead of about two yards. As the third American runner dashed up, Rudolph reached back to grab the relay baton, only to see the other woman drop it just short of her fingers. As Rudolph stooped and snatched the fumbled baton, the German runner surged to a commanding lead. Rudolph sprinted off in pursuit. To the astonishment of the crowd, Rudolph gained back all the ground she had lost and nipped across the finish line ahead of the German runner. Her effort earned her team the gold medal and set a new world record in the relay.

Wilma Rudolph had beat the odds, but that was not new for her. Born to a poor, black Tennessee family that already had fourteen children, Rudolph was sickly and underweight at birth and not expected to live. But she survived. Then, at age four, she was stricken with double pneumonia and scarlet fever. Once again, Rudolph pulled through, but her illness left her with a paralyzed left leg. Local doctors informed her parents that she would never walk again. Rudolph's determined mother took her daughter by bus to a clinic in Nashville. There they were told that with daily heat and water massages, the child might gradually gain a little use of her leg. Mrs. Rudolph worked six days a week as a maid and had no way to get her daughter to the clinic, so she taught herself and then her oldest children how to give the massage. For the next two years, Rudolph was given four massage treatments each day by family members. On Mrs. Rudolph's day off, she and her daughter made the forty-five-mile bus trip to Nashville for additional treatments. Since the family was too poor to afford a wheelchair, Rudolph spent her days confined to a bed or a chair.

Overcoming adversity

After two years with no progress, Rudolph suddenly began to regain some feeling in her leg. Two years later, she was able to walk with the aid of a leg brace. Just being able to walk a bit was not enough for Wilma Rudolph, however. She continued to exercise and was able to throw away the leg brace when she was eleven. At thirteen she tried out for the high school basketball team and at fifteen she was averaging over thirty-two points per game and was a member of the all-state team. Her basketball exploits brought her to the attention of the track coach at Tennessee State

Wilma Rudolph shows off her three gold medals from the 1960 Rome Olympics.

University and through his influence she became the first member of her family to attend college. Rudolph's triple gold in Rome was only the next step in a twenty-year-long race from behind to overcome seemingly unbeatable obstacles.

Determined to succeed

Not all obstacles are physical. Adversity can take many forms, as the linked stories of Olympic divers Dr. Sammy Lee and Greg Louganis show. Lee was the winner of the gold medal in platform diving and the bronze medal in springboard diving in 1948 and the gold medal in platform diving again in 1952. When Lee captured his second gold medal in 1952 at the age of thirty-two, he went into the record books as the oldest athlete ever to win an Olympic diving medal, but that is not even close to the true measure of his achievement.

Lee was born in California to Korean parents who had fled the Japanese invasion of Korea. Lee's family was too poor to attend the 1932 Games in Los Angeles, but when his father explained what the Olympics were all about, the boy announced that one day he would be an Olympic champion. "In what sport?" laughed his father. "Gee, I don't know, Pop," the boy replied, "but someday I'll find one." Not long afterward, Lee discovered that he could do things off a diving board that the other kids could not do. Soon he had heavier kids double-bouncing him off the diving board so he could get higher into the air and do more stunts. Diving was fast becoming Lee's passion.

Dealing with discrimination

In 1936, two things happened that cemented young Lee's determination. The gold medal winner in the marathon was a runner named Kitei Son. Although he was listed as Japanese and run-

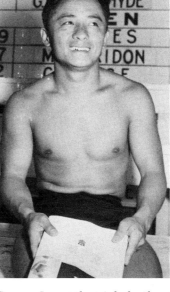

Sammy Lee at the trials for the 1948 London Olympic Games. Lee competed in the platform diving event.

ning for the Japanese team, Korean-Americans knew that Kitei Son was really Sohn Kee Chung, a Korean forced by the invading Japanese to compete for them. On the victory stand, Chung tore off his Japanese emblem and announced to the world, "I'm Korean, not Japanese." He was immediately seized and whisked away by the Japanese, but not before he had become a hero to Koreans everywhere and especially to young Sammy Lee. The other 1936 Olympian who made an indelible impression on Lee was the black American runner Jesse Owens. Owens had overcome racial prejudice at home and abroad to run brilliantly in the 1936 Olympics. Smarting under the widespread prejudice against Asians in this country, Lee was inspired by Owens's feats and the respect they brought to him.

At the 1948 London Olympic Games, Sammy Lee won the gold medal in the platform diving competition.

As a teenager, Lee had difficulty finding pools that would allow him to practice. The public pool in his hometown of Pasadena, California, for example, was open to him only on Mondays. Mondays were designated International Day, when non-whites were allowed to use the facilities. Each Monday evening, it was rumored, the pool was drained and then refilled with clean water. While still a teenager, Lee met and began to train with some of the best divers in the country, among them several former Olympians. One former champion—Farid Simaika, the Egyptian 1928 silver medalist who had moved to this country—gave Lee a piece of advice that he took to heart. He told the young diver that he might encounter prejudice in competition because he was of Korean descent. Simaika told Lee he would simply have to work twice as hard as other athletes. "You've got to be so much better that they have to give you the medal," Simaika said.

Competition and a continuing commitment

Lee began to perfect more complex dives than had ever before been done in competition—forward three-and-a-half somersaults, reverse two-and-a-half somersaults and inward two-and-a-half somersaults. Despite his growing success as a diver and his impressive academic achievements, prejudice pursued Lee even to the Olympic Games themselves. In London in 1948, just as Lee began competition in the platform diving competition, he was told that an American swimming association official had been heard telling the diving judges, "I hope you don't favor that Korean." Only Lee's extraordinary confidence and self-control could have enabled him to make one perfect dive after another off that thirty-three-foot diving tower with those vicious words of his fellow countryman ringing in his ears.

Olympic diver Greg Louganis with his coach, former Olympic gold medalist, Sammy Lee.

Lee won a second gold medal in 1952 in Helsinki, Finland. Although this marked his last Olympic performance, it did not end his close ties to the Olympics. Lee later took time from his medical career to coach a young man named Greg Louganis. Louganis had suffered from a difficult childhood. He was born of Samoan and Swedish parents who gave him up for adoption at birth. He was called nigger by his schoolmates in California because of his dark skin and labeled retarded because he had a severe reading disability called dyslexia. By age thirteen, Louganis was in trouble with the law and addicted to drugs and alcohol. But he also had developed an interest in diving. Lee spotted Louganis diving one day and saw promise in the young man's dives. With Lee's support, Louganis escaped from his difficulties into the world of competitive diving. He showed such promise that he qualified for the Montreal, Canada, Olympics at the age of sixteen. In Montreal in 1976, he finished sixth in the springboard

After winning a second gold medal in platform diving, Dr. Sammy Lee congratulates the other medalists at the 1952 Helsinki Olympic Games.

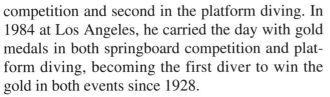

Greg Louganis performing a dive while training for the 1988 Olympics. Louganis won gold medals in both the springboard and platform diving competitions at the 1984 Los Angeles Olympics.

competition and second in the platform diving. In 1984 at Los Angeles, he carried the day with gold medals in both springboard competition and platform diving, becoming the first diver to win the gold in both events since 1928.

The Seoul Olympics in 1988 represented the third and last appearance in a long and remarkable career for Greg Louganis, and the Games provided a fitting conclusion. By 1988, at twenty-eight years old, Louganis was an old man in diving circles, but he was still the favorite in both diving events. Things began very badly, however, in the preliminaries of the springboard competition. Louganis bounced hard on the board and launched himself high into the air for a two-and-a-half pike. As he twisted and rolled and then plunged back toward the water, his head slammed into the end of the diving board. Spectators and television viewers alike will never forget the loud, hollow sound of Louganis's head hitting the board, the splash as he tumbled into the water, or the suspenseful moments as everyone waited to see if he would surface. Incredibly, Louganis suffered only an ugly gash in his scalp that was closed with five stitches. He immediately returned to competition and still managed to qual-

Sonja Henie used her ballet training to create her own style of figure skating which helped her to win gold medals at the 1928, 1932, and 1936 Olympics.

By perfecting turns, jumps, and twists on the ice, Sonja Henie won three consecutive Olympic gold medals and ten consecutive world championships in figure skating.

ify for the finals. He carried off both gold medals again and became the first man ever to repeat as Olympic champion in both events.

Taking a sport to new levels

In the drive to achieve victory, some athletes study, change, and improve on the skills and techniques employed in a sport. In doing so, these athletes transform their sports and raise them to new levels of competition.

Among the figure skaters at the 1924 Winter Olympics in Chamonix, France, was an eleven-year-old Norwegian girl named Sonja Henie. Henie did not do well in the competition, and she returned home determined to win a gold medal four years later. She threw herself into training, looking for dramatic moves that would raise the level of her skating. She took up ballet, which gave her physical strength and an array of powerful leaps, twists, and jumps that other skaters lacked. During the 1920s, figure skating was a rather slow, placid, waltzlike competition in which skaters demonstrated their poise and grace. Using her studies in ballet, Henie invented dozens of new turns, jumps, and twists on the ice, turning her performance into a fast, dazzling display of athletic power. In three years, she had captured the world figure skating championship, and she went

Sonja Henie's dramatic moves raised the level of performance in figure skating.

on to win it ten consecutive times. Her performance in the Olympics at St. Moritz, Switzerland, in 1928 earned Henie the gold medal. She earned gold medals again in 1932 and 1936. Her skill, imagination, and athletic ability had pushed figure skating to an entirely new level of performance.

An Olympic medalist represents the absolute pinnacle of athletic achievement. While every Olympic athlete began with some gift of physical talent, great or small, not one of them arrived at the Olympics without a struggle to shape and develop that talent. Each applied enormous confidence, determination, will power, and intelligence to use his or her talent and discipline to the greatest advantage. Olympic competition and achievement show all of us just how much an individual is capable of achieving through a union of physical and mental effort. The achievements of Olympic athletes give us standards to admire and emulate in our own lives.

4

Olympic Politics

ALTHOUGH THE OLYMPIC Games were conceived by Baron de Coubertin as a means to avoid or overcome international disagreements and distrust, they have not always achieved this ideal. National and international politics have interfered in the Games many times over the years. This interference has taken many forms. Political squabbles, nationalistic bias, violence, war, and bold efforts at turning the Games into propaganda for a particular cause have all tainted the Games at one time or another. Many nations, and even the Olympic organizers, have used the Games as a tool for punishment and persuasion. Politics has not destroyed de Coubertin's ideal, but it has many times strained his wish for an event that fosters international peace and friendship.

Nationalistic bias

Without knowing it at the time, de Coubertin himself planted the seed for some of the Olympic movement's greatest continuing problems. By organizing competitors into national teams, and celebrating victories based on country affiliation, de Coubertin placed an emphasis on rivalry and national pride. During the opening ceremonies, each team marches into the stadium behind its nation's flag. During the medal ceremonies, the national anthem of the gold medalist is played, while the

(opposite page) Adolf Hitler salutes the athletes at the 1936 Berlin Olympic Games.

61

American boxer Roy Jones is lifted off the ground by Park Si Hun, the South Korean boxer who defeated him during the 1988 Seoul Olympics. The decision was controversial. Some people believed the judges had been bribed by the South Koreans.

flag of the winning athlete's nation is run up a flagpole in the stadium. Flags of the nations of the silver and bronze medalists are displayed to the left and right and slightly below. At the closing ceremonies, the national teams once again parade around the stadium behind their flag bearers. Olympic athletes compete not only for themselves but also for their countries. These practices reinforce the division of nations and sometimes lead to disputes over nationalistic bias in the Games.

In the early years of the modern Olympics, the host country provided the officials and judges for all of the events. This proved to be a problem because these officials and judges often favored athletes from their own countries. Later, when officiating was taken out of the hands of host countries, complaints of bias still surfaced.

Of course, in any sporting event, there are bound to be a few who will question the fairness of judges' and officials' rulings. Even for those present at an event, it is sometimes hard to determine what really happened.

In the 1988 Olympics in Seoul, South Korea, nationalistic fervor was blamed by some for a highly controversial boxing decision. In that match, American boxer Roy Jones appeared to be a runaway winner, according to some observers. But the judges gave the decision to South Korean boxer Park Si Hun. The decision prompted angry responses from Americans and other people in boxing circles. They accused unnamed Koreans of possibly bribing officials to score in favor of the Korean boxer. "All during the tournament, we kept hearing about the South Koreans being all over some judges, taking them out to dinner, giving them gifts," one tournament boxing judge told the *Los Angeles Times*. The Koreans denied any wrongdoing and accused the Americans of an unsportsmanlike reaction to a lost match.

Using the Games for propaganda

At various times during the history of the Olympics, nations and political groups have tried to use the Games to boost a cause or point of view. With its worldwide audience of millions, the Olympics provide a unique opportunity to present a message that will be heard around the globe. All host nations hope for smoothly run Games that will impress other nations. But some countries have tried to leave more than good impressions. Some have sought to use the Olympics to win the

Adolf Hitler at a Nazi rally. By 1936, the Nazi party controlled Germany, and Hitler wanted to prove his theory of Aryan superiority at the Berlin Olympics.

world's support for a particular way of life.

In 1931, when the International Olympic Committee chose the German cities of Garmisch-Partenkirchen and Berlin to host the 1936 Winter and Summer Games, no one could have predicted that five years later Germany would be in the hands of Adolf Hitler and his Nazi party. By 1936, Hitler's regime was in full control of Germany. He had announced that the Games would demonstrate to the world the superiority of the Germans and the inferiority of blacks and Jews whom he referred to as "mongrel races."

From the start, Nazi racist policies caused problems for the Olympics. When the teams arrived in Garmisch-Partenkirchen, they discovered signs reading "Dogs and Jews Are Not Allowed" posted on the toilet facilities at the Olympic sites. IOC president Comte Henri de Baillet-Latour requested an immediate meeting with Hitler. "Mr. Chancellor," he protested, "the signs are not in conformity with Olympic principles." Hitler replied, "Mr. President, when you are invited to a friend's home, you don't tell him how to run it, do you?" Baillet-Latour's response reflects the idealism of the Olympic movement and the IOC's absolute determination that the Games not be used for purposes of political propaganda. "Mr. Chancellor," he replied, "when the five-circled flag is raised over the stadium, it is no longer Germany. It is Olympia, and we are masters here." The signs came down.

Olympics in Berlin

The Berlin Games opened on August 1 with an impressive torch-lighting ceremony before a capacity crowd of 110,000 spectators. Approximately five thousand athletes were on hand from fifty-three nations. The traditional marching order of the nations at the Olympic opening ceremonies places Greece first, followed by the other nations in alphabetical order in the language of the host country. As the teams filed around the track in Berlin, those sympathetic to the Nazi cause saluted Hitler's box with the Nazi salute. Representatives from other nations marched past with eyes averted. The United States team was greeted with whistles, jeers, and vile insults directed at its Jewish and black members.

The first gold medals of the Games were awarded to the German shot-putter Hans Woellke. Following the medal ceremony, Woellke was paraded with great fanfare to Hitler's official box

German citizens beg Adolf Hitler for his autograph as he sits in his official box overlooking the Olympic Games.

to be personally congratulated by his *fuehrer*, or grand leader. Winners from several other nations were given the same treatment. Then came the high jump. The first- and second-place finishers were Cornelius Johnson and Dave Albritton, both black Americans. As the two athletes received their awards, there was a stir in the official box. Hitler and his party were quickly leaving the stadium. The official explanation was that it was late in the day and it looked like rain. It was clear to everyone, however, that the German dictator was avoiding the humiliation of congratulating two black men for athletic victories because their victories disproved his theories about the inferiority of their race.

Shattering Nazi myths

The next day, and in the days that followed, the German leader showed a bit more caution. Winners were no longer paraded to the official box. Hitler retired to a room beneath the stadium to deliver his thanks to German winners. While this avoided the public embarrassment of acknowledging the victories of those he viewed as inferior, it could not hide how completely the German plans to use the Games for propaganda purposes had failed. On the field, German theories of racial superiority were being refuted. No one brought this point home more clearly than runner Jesse Owens of the United States.

Owens was the son of an Alabama cotton picker and the grandson of a black slave. A naturally gifted runner, Owens attracted national attention while he was still very young. During high school, he won easy victories in national track-and-field events and set a record of 9.4 seconds in the 100-yard dash—a record that lasted more than twenty years. In college at Ohio State University, Owens tied the world record for the 100-

Jesse Owens and Helen Stephens, two black members of the 1936 U.S. Olympic team.

Jesse Owens takes off in the 400-yard relay at a meet in White City, Britain after winning four gold medals at the Olympics.

yard dash and set world records in the long jump, the 220-yard low hurdles, and the 220-yard dash. His long-jump record held for twenty-five years. So, Owens was well-prepared for competition in the 1936 Olympics. He competed at the Olympics in four events. He set or equaled Olympic records nine times during preliminary and final competition and won gold medals in the 100-meter dash, the 200-meter dash, the broad jump, and the 400-meter relay. Fourteen years later, sportswriters across the country would vote Owens the best male athlete in fifty years. While he certainly was the best male athlete in at least fifty years, even more significant in the public mind was the role he played in shattering German plans for a great propaganda victory at the Berlin Games.

Jesse Owens completes the broad jump that won him the gold medal at the 1936 Berlin Olympics.

Political ideology has found its way into the Games in other ways. Nations, and even private organizations, have used boycotts and the threat of boycotts as tools for persuasion and punishment. The Olympic Games usually bring money and prestige to host countries and the nations that take part. By pulling out of the Olympics and sometimes convincing others to do the same, nations deny money and prestige to the targets of their boycotts. Boycotts nearly always have an added effect. They tarnish the Olympic image and reduce the number of competitors.

The two most destructive boycotts the Olympics have experienced were the back-to-back American and Soviet boycotts of 1980 and 1984. In the spring of 1980, following the Soviet invasion of Afghanistan, President Jimmy Carter announced that the United States would boycott the Summer Games, which were to be held in

Moscow that year. Carter called for the boycott as an expression of his displeasure with the invasion and succeeded in applying pressure on fifty-five other nations to do the same. The governments of some of the United States' closest allies, such as Great Britain and Australia, supported the boycott officially but did not stop athletes from traveling to Moscow as individuals. Carter allowed no such choice. He threatened to revoke the passport of any American athlete who traveled to the Soviet Union for the Games.

Soviet response

The Soviets were deeply angered by the boycott. The Moscow Games were to have provided the Soviets an opportunity to demonstrate that they could match the outstanding performance of their athletes with their skills as hosts. Because of the U.S.-led boycott, however, the number of nations competing and the number of athletes present were lower than they had been in nearly three decades.

Although the Moscow Games produced more world records than had been set four years earlier in Montreal, many of these records were later overturned in other competitions by athletes whose nations had boycotted the Games.

It came as no surprise that the Soviets reciprocated with their own boycott four years later when the Summer Olympics moved to Los Angeles. On May 8, 1984, less than three months before the Games were to begin, the Soviets announced that they would not attend. By the end of that week, Bulgaria, East Germany, Vietnam, Mongolia, Czechoslovakia, Laos, Afghanistan, Hungary, Poland, Cuba, and North Korea had joined the boycott. Just as it had in Moscow four years earlier, athletic competition suffered.

In the history of the Olympic Games, the Moscow Games of 1980 and the Los Angeles

President Jimmy Carter threatened to revoke the passport of any American athlete who traveled to the Soviet Union for the 1980 Olympic Games.

Black South Africans protest their government's apartheid policies. South Africa had been banned from participation in the Games because of these policies. In July 1991, South Africa was readmitted to the Olympics after key apartheid laws were repealed.

Games of 1984 will remain low points for the Olympics and the Games' constant—and often fruitless—struggle to remain unaffected by politics.

Using the Olympics to force reform

Nations are not alone in their use of the Olympics for political ends. The IOC has more than once banned a country from participation to make a political statement. South Africa, for example, has been banned from participation in the Games for several decades because of its apartheid policies. Under South Africa's apartheid policies, which separate the races, black South Africans are denied the freedom to vote, live, and work as they choose. South Africa had been a continuous participant in the Olympics since 1906, and South African athletes had gathered their fair share of medals. By the late 1950s, however, public pressure was so great that the IOC could no longer ignore the fact that a nation whose population was predominantly black was represented by all-white teams. Apartheid policies also allowed white athletes in South Africa to enjoy excellent facilities and highly organized sports activities, while black South Africans were deprived of athletic training facilities and given no opportunity to compete either nationally or internationally. The apartheid policies even required other nations' teams coming to compete in South Africa to leave their black athletes at home. In 1962, the IOC warned South Africa that it faced expulsion from the Olympics unless it ceased its discriminatory policies. Over the next two years, deadlines came and went, and still South Africa did not comply. The country was banned from participation in the 1964 Tokyo Games.

In early 1968, the IOC voted to reinstate South Africa to Olympic competition, based on a report that said that progress was being made in preparing an integrated team. In the following weeks, one nation after another announced that it would withdraw from competition if the South African team competed. By the time the total had reached forty countries, the IOC realized it had no choice, and it revoked South Africa's invitation. Since that time, the question of reinstating South Africa has been raised regularly, and each time a storm of protest and threats of international boycott has immediately followed. During this time, a few South African athletes, both white and black, have managed to compete, despite the ban, by temporarily becoming citizens of other countries and competing on their Olympic teams. In July 1991, however, the IOC readmitted South Africa to the Olympics after the government repealed key apartheid laws. This opens the door for South African athletes to participate in the 1992 Olympic Games.

Terrorism in the Olympics

As the Olympic Games moved through the 1960s and into the 1970s, the international news was dominated more and more frequently by acts of political violence and terrorism. Airplanes and boats were hijacked by terrorist groups, and political figures were kidnapped and assassinated. It was inevitable that sooner or later some group would attempt to use violence at the Games to make a political statement.

No attempt to use the Olympics as a political weapon equals the horrible events at the Munich Olympics of 1972. On September 5, the eleventh day of competition, a group of black-masked Palestinians slipped into the Olympic Village, kidnapped nine Israeli athletes, and killed two others. While millions of television viewers around the world looked on, the masked gunmen demanded the release of two hundred imprisoned Arabs held by Israeli authorities. They also sought safe transportation for themselves and their hostages out of the country. After a long day of negotiations with German authorities, at dusk the terrorists and their hostages were carried by helicopter to a nearby airfield. An announcement was made that the hostages were to be released there. Because of a news blackout, it was not until the following morning that the tragic story of the subsequent events was told. At the airport, a gun battle broke out. When the guns were stilled, all nine Israeli athletes were dead, along with a German policeman and five of the terrorists.

In the face of this great tragedy, many people thought that the rest of the Munich Games should be canceled. However, after deliberation, the IOC announced that the Games would continue. IOC members believed that if terrorists were allowed to force cancellation of the Games, the Olympic movement might never recover. So, after a memorial service attended by eighty thousand people, the Games continued.

During the 1972 Munich Olympics, a Palestinian terrorist looks out of an Olympic village apartment where he is keeping the Israeli Olympians hostage.

Baron de Coubertin had hoped that the Olympic festival would stand apart from political disputes. Until recently the IOC claimed to be unaffected by political considerations or pressures when making its rulings and decisions. Despite these claims, national and international events outside the Games have at times had a major influence on their planning and conduct. Although the Olympic ideals have suffered a number of hard blows in situations such as those described here, the Olympic ideals themselves are strong enough to have enabled the festival to survive. Based on the experiences of the past, it appears that the nations of the world are gradually learning from their mistakes, learning that the Olympic Games and the ideals they represent are too important to be distorted or destroyed for political ends.

Armed police move to a terrace at the back of the Olympic village apartment where Palestinian terrorists are holding the Israeli Olympians hostage.

5

The Limits of Fair Competition . . . and Beyond

MANY FORMS OF competition including the Olympics, have suffered from cheating and unsportsmanlike conduct of one sort or another. Although Olympic athletes are extraordinarily talented and extremely disciplined people, they suffer the same temptations and pressures as everyone else. Success in Olympic competition can bring great public acclaim and large financial rewards, and this increases the temptations and the pressure.

Rigging events

Sometimes an athlete's lapse in good sportsmanship is momentary and occurs in the heat of competition. Over the years, disqualifications for intentional pushing, shoving, and fouls have been a regular but infrequent part of events at the Olympic Games. Sometimes, however, the cheating is cooly planned and premeditated. One imaginative method of cheating was uncovered in the fencing competition in Montreal in 1976. In the fencing competition, two opponents battle with light swords in a fast-moving, complicated series

(opposite page) Ben Johnson parades around the track after setting a new world record and winning the gold medal for the men's 100-meter race at the 1988 Seoul Olympic Games. After Johnson tested positive for steroids, competitor Carl Lewis was awarded the medal.

Fencing competitors wear electrically wired suits that register a hit when an opponent's sword touches them.

of offensive and defensive moves. Points are awarded for each successful contact with the opponent. The athletes and their weapons are wired, and each contact between one athlete's sword and the other's body armor is registered electronically. During one match, Boris Onischenko of the Soviet Union lunged at his opponent, stumbled, and missed. Mysteriously, a hit registered on the scoreboard. The judges quickly confiscated Onischenko's sword and discovered that he had rewired it to send contact signals whenever he pushed a concealed button. Onischenko was disqualified and barred from further competition.

Not all cheating is as obvious as this. Usually,

in fact, it is a matter of interpretation. Rarely do both sides agree on what occurred when cheating is an issue. The same goes for unsportsmanlike conduct. In the heat of competition, it is often difficult to judge whether an illegal act was deliberate or accidental and sometimes even referees have a hard time judging whether a particular move was illegal. Accusations of cheating and unsportsmanlike conduct surface often, much as they did after the American-Soviet basketball game at the 1972 Munich Olympics. Following their 51-50 loss to the Soviets, the Americans contended they had been cheated of victory by sloppy officiating and a series of illegal moves on the court.

In the final seconds of the game, the Americans contended, the Soviets pulled a series of illegal moves that would not have been allowed in a third-grade school-yard game. An American guard attempting to block an in-bounds pass was interfered with by one of the referees. The Soviet passer stepped over the line before he made his in-bounds pass. A Soviet forward was waiting illegally under the basket, inside the three-second lane. Two U.S. players were guarding him. He knocked them both down, leaped for the ball, turned, and sank the basket. But the buzzer sounded and the game ended. The United States immediately filed an appeal. An appointed panel of judges decided in favor of the Soviet team, which took home a gold medal. U.S. team members voted unanimously to refuse their silver medals.

Resorting to drugs

In recent years, the focus on unsportsmanlike conduct has shifted from physical tricks to chemical assistance. Many kinds of chemical stimulants available to athletes temporarily increase

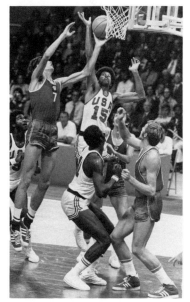

The Soviet Union tries for a basket during the Olympic basketball final between the U.S. and the USSR. The Soviets won by one point, but the Americans and one of the referees contested the decision, saying that the winning basket was scored after the buzzer sounded the end of the game.

physical performance by speeding up reaction time and boosting endurance and stamina. There is also a class of drugs called steroids, which help an athlete artificially increase muscle tissue and physical strength. While stimulants and steroids can improve athletic performance, both also can be harmful to the body, especially in large doses or taken over a long period of time. Stimulants can cause severe over-reactions and even death. Steroid use can cause physical problems, including liver damage and harmful changes in the cardiovascular system. Steroid users often experience extreme personality changes and frequently exhibit violent behavior.

Serious official concern about the use of chemicals to enhance performance in Olympic events is fairly recent. Historians say athletes of the ancient Olympics frequently used stimulants—chiefly alcohol and herbs—to improve athletic performance. During the early modern Olympics, official attitude toward the use of stimulants was lax. At the 1904 Games in St. Louis, for example, J.T. Hickes, the gold-medal winner in the marathon, took doses of brandy and shots of strychnine while he ran. All through the 1900s, world-class cyclists regularly used caffeine, nitroglycerine, heroin, and cocaine to improve their speed and endurance. At the 1952 Winter Games in Oslo, Norway, the floor of the speed skaters' changing room was littered with used syringes and broken glass vials, which had contained various chemicals injected by skaters for enhancing their performances.

Drugs cause an Olympic death

While the IOC had been aware and concerned about drug use for several decades, an incident at the 1960 Games in Rome caused it to take official action. During the 100-kilometer bicycle race,

Knut Enemark Jensen at the beginning of the 100-kilometer Olympic race during the 1960 Rome Olympics. The Danish cyclist collapsed and died at the end of the race due to the drugs he had taken to increase his speed and stamina.

Knut Enemark Jensen, a Danish cyclist, collapsed on the track and died. At first his death was attributed to heat and sunstroke. An autopsy soon revealed, however, that death was due to a mixture of amphetamines and other drugs he had taken before the race to increase his stamina and speed. The IOC took steps at this point to eliminate drugs from Olympic competition, although success would prove elusive. An Olympic Medical Commission was established specifically to check competitors for drugs. Routine drug testing began at the Tokyo Games in 1964 and has continued to the present. With the passing years, however, the illegal materials available to athletes have become more sophisticated and harder to detect.

During the 1960s and the early 1970s, official concern was chiefly directed toward stimulants designed to increase a competitor's physical output. By 1976, the IOC had compiled a list of more than thirty forbidden substances. It routinely tested for these substances in the bodies of Olympic athletes. By the late 1970s, concern had shifted to the use of steroids to artificially build up an athlete's body tissue and muscles. Steroid use is difficult to detect; all traces of the drug are

Because of steroid use, American weight lifter Mark Cameron was disqualified from the 1976 Montreal Olympics. He was the first Olympic athlete to test positive for steroid use.

usually flushed from the body within a matter of days after the last treatment. The muscle tissue added with the drug's help remains much longer. Many people involved in athletics have long suspected that the few athletes caught using steroids every four years represent only the tip of the iceberg of steroid use. Medical and legal experts interviewed by the *New York Times* have estimated that at least half of the nine thousand athletes who competed at the 1988 Olympics in Seoul, South Korea, had used steroids in training.

Detecting steroids

The first Olympic athlete to test positive for steroids was American weight lifter Mark Cameron. Cameron was disqualified from the 1976 Montreal Olympics because of steroid use. Since then, steroids have been detected in others. The athlete who perhaps gained the greatest attention for steroid use was Canadian runner Ben Johnson.

The 100-meter race between Johnson and Carl Lewis of the United States was to be the highlight of the 1988 Olympic track competition in Seoul. In 1984 at Los Angeles, Lewis had become the first athlete to equal Jesse Owens's 1936 feat of four track-and-field gold medals in a single Olympics and was hoping to do it again in 1988. Johnson had taken bronze medals in two of those races but was favored to win in 1988 because he had captured the 100-meter world record the year before at an international meet.

The 100-meter race at Seoul was fast and close, but Johnson put on a spectacular burst of speed at the end and overturned his own 9.83-seconds record with a time of 9.79 seconds. Lewis finished a fraction of a step and .13 seconds behind. Johnson's triumph was short-lived, however. Routine drug testing that afternoon revealed the presence

Ben Johnson sprints to the finish during his 100-meter race at the 1988 Seoul Olympics.

of steroids in Johnson's body. Punishment was swift. The next morning, the IOC executive council found Johnson guilty of violating its rules against performance-enhancing drugs. It disqualified his performance and awarded the gold medal to Lewis. Given the Olympics' major drug-testing program, it was hard for people to believe that Johnson or his trainers could have hoped to escape detection. Indeed, for a short time, Johnson and his trainers claimed that someone had tampered with Johnson's test sample. The case against the Canadian athlete was too strong to be denied for long, however, and he departed quickly from Seoul in disgrace.

The effects of Olympic drug regulation

While investigators would eventually conclude that Johnson and his trainers were completely aware of what they were doing, the question on everyone's mind was why they did it and how many others might be doing the same. An article in the Canadian national magazine *MacLean's* noted that Olympic victory was becoming too important and too financially rewarding for athletes or countries to leave the competition to skill alone. "In 1970, Ottawa, Canada, spent $5 million to subsidize sports. By 1978, the budget was $30 million and by Seoul it was untraceable in the stratosphere. . . ." The Olympics were no longer just a gathering of athletes but a means of bringing big money to nations and their competitors.

In 1990, the IOC announced that it would lift Ben Johnson's suspension in time for him to train and compete in the 1992 Games in Barcelona, Spain. A noticeably slimmer, less muscular-looking Johnson began to make appearances at national and international events. How the public and other athletes will perceive Johnson's rapid reinstatement remains to be seen. Although John-

A poster of Ben Johnson lies in a trash can after he tested positive for drug use and lost his gold medal.

son's disqualification was the big news maker, he was not the only Olympic athlete to fail a drug test in Seoul. Two U.S. athletes, Angel Meyers on the swim team and Steve Hegg, the 1984 gold- and silver-medal-winning cyclist, had been eliminated from the team before it arrived in Seoul because of failed drug tests. In the days before Johnson's disqualification, two Bulgarian weight lifters were stripped of their gold medals after failing drug tests, and the entire Bulgarian team departed for home rather than face further tests. Altogether, during the Seoul Games, nine athletes from six nations tested positive for drugs; four of them were medalists.

The best hope that the Olympics has of overcoming cheating in any form, and drug abuse in particular, is with fair officiating, rigorous testing for drugs, and ultimately with the athletes themselves. While there will always be an occasional individual who will succumb to temptation or fail to withstand pressure, most Olympic competitors want their victory to be clean and fair.

6

The Olympic Games and the Olympic Athletes —Today and Tomorrow

IF AN ANCIENT Greek athlete were to have suddenly been transported from the stadium at the foot of Mount Olympus into the midst of the modern Olympic Games, that athlete might be momentarily confused, but would find that in most ways Olympic ideals have remained unchanged. The ancient Greek would probably agree also that the Games were still having a hard time remaining completely true to their ideals. A recent article in *Sports Illustrated* magazine painted the picture quite accurately: "There have always been two Olympics. One is the concern of the organizers, the politicians, the sellers, the television people, the crowds nursing their vicarious passions. The other is simpler. It's an athlete in the arena, facing the best in the world. It's a chance to test yourself in that crushing ultimate pressure, to see if you can take it and still sum-

Sir Michael Morris became president of the International Olympic Committee in 1972, and began to work to solve the problems of the modern Olympics.

mon your best. That crucible is what creates the bonds, what transcends ideologies."

In 1996, the modern Olympics celebrate its centennial year. The Games are a venerable institution now, and no matter how they may be altered, it seems assured that Baron de Coubertin's dream of a truly international sports festival will not die. There are major forces at work at present, however, that may change the face of the Olympics in the future. In 1972, as he took over the presidency of the IOC, Sir Michael Morris, Lord Killian of Ganty Galway, Ireland, summed up the status of the Olympic Games and their future very neatly: "The future of the Olympic movement is, I believe, assured, although we always have our problems. Among these are the immense growth of the Games; amateurism and eligibility; political interference; and the use of scientific advances in medicine."

Dealing with money problems

The world being what it is, politics in some form or other will probably always shadow the Olympics. This means Olympic organizers will have to be vigilant in guarding against its intrusion in the Games. What troubles some in Olympic circles more is the immense growth of the Games. Over the years, Olympic organizers have added dozens of sports, nations, and athletes to the Olympic schedule. Some people worry that by adding even more events and lengthening the time span of the Games, eventually the Olympics will cease being a single festival. In its place will be a series of international meets strung together with no unifying theme. Athletes will come and go for their own particular events, destroying the camaraderie that has characterized the Games since their revival in 1896.

Financing the Games

Because of their growth, financing the Olympic Games has proved to be a challenge in recent decades. In the 1960s and 1970s, there was a period when it appeared that the days of the Games might be nearing an end simply because no one could afford to host them any longer. The first modern Olympic Games cost nowhere near the $30 million spent for the 1960 Summer Games in Rome, Italy. When the Games moved to Tokyo in 1964, the Japanese government spent $2.7 billion without complaint. Mexico City spent a modest $175 million on the Games four years later. When the Canadian government tried to produce a modest Olympics eight years after that in Montreal, however, their planned budget of $310 million ballooned to $1.2 billion because of poor planning, labor strikes, and staggering inflation. Despite the prestige and earnings from hosting the Olympics, many cities and countries did not have this kind of money to spend. Host cities and countries began looking for other ways of paying for the Games.

When the Olympics came to Los Angeles in 1984, they were staged for the first time com-

Advertising helped finance the 1984 Los Angeles Olympics. Pictured here is a torch runner who was sponsored by AT&T.

pletely without government financing. The United States Olympic Committee and the City of Los Angeles adopted a completely different plan. The entire sports festival was paid for by private sponsors and by money generated by the Games themselves. Major U.S. and international corporations were encouraged to make large contributions in return for being allowed to use their association with the Games in their advertising and promotional materials. Single sponsors paid for the entire construction of several of the new facilities.

The organizers of the 1988 Winter Games in Calgary, Canada, took their cue from Los Angeles and signed lucrative corporate sponsorship deals. Sponsors paid over $67 million to the Calgary organizers and another $120 million to the IOC for rights to both the Winter and Summer Games. Calgary went into the record books as the first Winter Games ever to show a profit, estimated at $30 million at the close of the festival.

Even though the Games seem inclined toward expansion now, in the future, there is likely to be pressure to eliminate certain sports from the Olympic schedule. The money raised by selling the broadcasting rights to the Games presently

The advertisements plastered on the hockey rink in Lake Placid, New York at a pre-Olympics hockey match helped finance the 1984 Los Angeles Games.

Advertisers such as the Kodak-Eastman Company financed the 1984 Los Angeles Olympic Games.

pays for a large part of the Olympics. Already the scheduling of events is dictated by television's requirement that the most popular events take place during peak viewing hours. It must have already occurred to more than one television executive that if the popular events could be expanded and the unpopular ones eliminated, the broadcasting profits might be even greater.

Determining eligibility

Just as Olympic organizers face decisions on which sports to include, they also must wrestle with a continuing question of who should be allowed to compete. From the first modern Olympics in Athens, there have been questions and debates concerning the issue of eligibility.

In Athens, when two young English employees at the British Embassy entered their names to compete in the cycling events, they were at first refused a place on the British team. Since they belonged to the working class, they did not fit into the upper-class British sports definition of amateur. In that society at the time, an amateur was a gentleman, someone with an independent income. The IOC prevailed eventually, and the two men competed.

Baron de Coubertin's Olympic ideal embraced all classes, but his wish that Olympic athletes be completely free of the taint of financial reward presented problems from the beginning. As levels of athletic achievement rose, along with the time and expense required for proper training, it became more difficult for Olympic athletes to carry on their sport as a part-time affair or a hobby. For many years, the IOC tried to deal with the problem of eligibility by constantly sharpening and refining its definitions of amateur and professional. By and large, professional athletes were those who earned their living by playing their sport. Amateur athletes gained their livelihood by some means unrelated to their sport.

Redefining amateur athletics

As the decades have passed, the conflict between Olympic ideals and reality have become increasingly difficult to ignore. In the real world in many sports, competitors of Olympic caliber spend all of their time in training. They have no other occupation; their sport is their job. Whatever way their food, clothing, and shelter is provided for them, it comes as a direct result of practicing their sport. The amateur versus professional debate became a question of defining which means of providing support for athletes-in-training were acceptable and which were not. The IOC found itself devoting enormous time and energy resolving these questions as they applied to

Avery Brundage, former president of the Amateur Athletic Union, barred ski instructors from Olympic competition on the basis that they were professionals.

different sports and to different nations.

As early as 1936, when Avery Brundage was still president of the Amateur Athletic Union, he had succeeded in temporarily having all ski instructors barred from Olympic competition on the grounds that they were professionals. Many world-class skiers supported themselves by teaching skiing, and Brundage considered this a conflict with their amateur status. The International Ski Federation reacted by organizing its own world championships in direct competition with the Olympics in which instructors were allowed to compete. With many of the best skiers barred from competition, the Olympics suffered until 1946, when a compromise was worked out between the IOC and the Federation. It allowed those who gave elementary instruction to keep their amateur status.

This compromise did not last long. The IOC

Skiers often agree to wear advertising for companies so that they can support themselves while training for the Olympics.

continued to worry about athletes who turned themselves into professionals in everything but name. What the IOC was trying to root out now was not really professionalism but commercialization of amateur athletics. IOC officials frowned on athletes who turned a tidy profit from their sport because this seemed to destroy the spirit of amateur athletic competition. The worst offenders in this regard had always been world-class skiers. Ski equipment and clothing manufacturers had long been paying huge sums to Olympic skiers to wear and endorse their products. By 1972, it was estimated that the better European skiers were earning as much as fifty thousand dollars a year from promotions and endorsements.

As the line between the professional and the amateur athlete has become harder to draw, the IOC has shifted with the times. It has turned over all decisions concerning eligibility to individual sports federations, leaving the final decision as to who is an amateur and who is a professional to these independent sports organizations.

The popular and commercial success of the Olympics has also contributed to making Olympic competition a money-making proposition for the athletes. A successful competitor is almost unable to avoid profiting financially from his or her victory. And, as athletes are called on to train harder and longer and to use more sophisticated facilities in order to achieve higher standards of performance, the expense of remaining in competition grows higher. This, in turn, further blurs the issue of whether it is reasonable to expect Olympic athletes to truly remain amateurs.

Another eligibility question that the IOC may

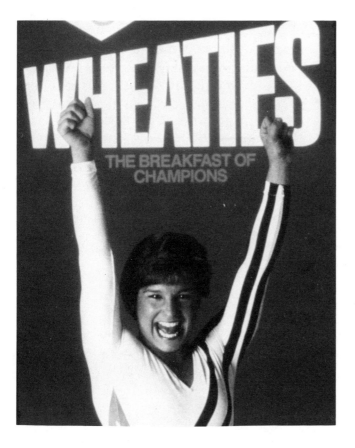

Olympic athletes can make a living by endorsing products. Mary Lou Retton earned thousands of dollars endorsing a variety of products after her participation in the Olympics. Here, Retton is pictured on a box of Wheaties.

Men and women compete together in Olympic yachting.

Terry Bankley, a skeet shooter on the 1988 U.S. team, is one of the few women to compete with men in the Olympics.

have to face in the future involves separate men's and women's competitions. At present there are only three Olympic sports in which men and women compete together: yachting, marksmanship, and the equestrian events. As women's performances have improved rapidly in many events and as women have gained more equal treatment in the general society, some women have demanded to compete equally with men in sports as well. The performance standards in women's events come closer to the men's with each passing Olympics. Many argue that all the women need in order to equal men's achievements is the stimulus of competing with them. On the other side, people argue that it will always be impossible for women to achieve records in events that are designed to exploit the basic physical differences between men and women. To allow women to compete equally with men, they say, will guarantee constant runner-up status to the women. This question of equality of the sexes may turn out to be the most difficult issue the Games have had to face.

The Olympic equestrian competition is one of three events in the Olympics in which women are allowed to compete alongside men.

Scientific advances in medicine will also pose difficult and interesting questions for the Olympic Games. Problems with illegal body-building steroids and performance-enhancing drugs in the past will likely prove to be nothing compared to what future advances in science and technology could bring. While the use of steroids to artificially increase muscle tissue has been clearly forbidden by Olympic rules for some time, another medical controversy that cropped up in 1976 in Montreal indicates the puzzling nature of controversies yet to come. Rumors circulated at Montreal that a number of athletes, including gold-medal-winning Finnish runner Lasse Viren, had engaged in a little-known practice called blood doping. This technique involves drawing off and storing several pints of the athlete's blood months before competition. The body naturally replaces the blood and, on the eve of competition, the stored blood is then injected into the athlete. Supposedly this increased blood volume gives the athlete more stamina and increased oxygen capacity. No one ever admitted to the practice, and it has never been determined that shooting oneself up with one's own blood is illegal. Rumors of blood doping have surfaced occasionally since 1976, but the IOC has taken no formal action.

The question of blood doping raises the issue of whether certain changes an athlete makes in his or her own body tissue can be considered illegal. What will be the ruling when competitors begin to undergo surgical procedures to reconstruct their bodies into stronger, more efficient athletic machines? Already, people with physical injuries and disabilities are having bones reinforced and lengthened. Grafts of muscle and nerve tissue are routine now for the injured and those suffering

Finnish runner Lasse Viren wins the gold medal for the men's five thousand meter race in the 1976 Montreal Olympics. The athlete has been accused of blood doping.

Scientific advances, like this artificial leg, are already helping people with disabilities compete in athletics. Some people worry that further advances might enable athletes to restructure or rebuild muscles and limbs to give them greater strength and endurance.

from diseases or birth defects. Professional and amateur athletes alike now routinely undergo surgical procedures that rebuild injured body parts. Soon they may be considering surgery to improve on what nature and training can give them. The idea of a "constructed" athlete may be hard to believe. Yet the future may find scientists designing athletes from scratch. It is not hard to believe, given what scientists are already doing with genetic manipulation in plants and animals, that sometime it may be possible to alter human genetic material in order to enhance athletic ability.

Regardless of how many groups claim a piece

of the Olympics for themselves—organizers, politicians, salespeople, media people, and spectators—the Olympic Games will always belong to the athletes and remain a testimonial to the determination of the human spirit.

As we watch spellbound the remarkable accomplishments of a swimmer like Mark Spitz or a skater like Brian Boitano, their talents and achievements might seem superhuman. But the significance of the Olympic Games is that its ideals—dedication, hard work, perseverance, and self-confidence—are ideals to which everyone can aspire. While the Olympic athletes described in this book and many other Olympians like them are extraordinarily gifted individuals, the quality that marks them as genuine Olympians is not the talent they were born with but the determination

Mark Spitz dives into the pool for his leg of the men's 4x100-meter relay. He won his seventh gold medal at the 1972 Munich Olympic Games for his performance in this race.

they have cultivated in themselves.

The story of Lany Robert Bassham, the silver medalist in the small-bore rifle competition in 1972 and the gold-medal winner in 1976, is a good example. As a boy, Bassham showed no particular physical ability or talent. "From childhood on, I always wanted to be a winner," he said. "I'd run in all the races, but I'd always lose. No matter how hard I tried and no matter how early I showed up for practice, I never was able to do much. At the same time I was infatuated with the Olympics. I read all the books about the Games, and I pictured myself being an Olympic athlete of some sort. It wasn't important which event—just to be in the Games was the thing. Unfortunately, I was slow, short, and clumsy. I also had no natural ability. I tried out for baseball and got alternate right fielder. In basketball I sat on the far end of the bench. And I was just too small for football."

Finding a way to excel

When a friend happened to mention that he was on a rifle team and that shooting was an Olympic event, Bassham decided he could excel at the sport. He began shooting when he was twelve. Before he was even in high school he was a national champion. After college Bassham joined the Army as a second lieutenant and became a member of the Army rifle team, training with and competing against the best international sharpshooters. In 1972 Bassham made the U.S. Olympic team. Although he felt the gold medal was within his reach, he ended up with a silver medal after letting his nerves get the better of him.

Bassham spent the next four years studying Olympic medalists to find out how they managed the pressure of competition and then prepared himself for the 1976 Games. This time the prepa-

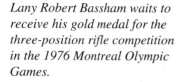

Lany Robert Bassham waits to receive his gold medal for the three-position rifle competition in the 1976 Montreal Olympic Games.

ration paid off. Despite stiff competition and tense final rounds, Bassham won the gold medal.

Years later, Bassham reflected on the qualities that made him an Olympic champion and shaped his life. "I feel very blessed and I thank the good Lord for allowing me to have this kind of life. I don't know why things have happened to me the way they have, but I appreciate the parents I've had, the people I've known . . . the opportunity to have trained with the best. I'm even happy with my failure in 1972. I think if I had won then there's no way I would be as well off as I am today. I wouldn't have searched things out. If I had won, I might be a young lieutenant colonel. . . . Not that there's anything wrong with being a lieutenant colonel, but now I have a richer life because I failed in 1972. So I have a message: don't give up when you run into a wall. There's a way around it. And maybe there's a reason why you have to find your way around, through, or over that wall."

The modern Olympic Games are about breaking around, through, or over walls—walls that divide people, walls that separate nations, and the physical and mental walls that hold back an individual from becoming something better than he or she is. The history of the Olympics is the story of these walls being broken over and over again by every single one of the thousands of competitors who have entered Olympic stadiums all around the globe—Olympians every one.

Glossary

amateur: A person who engages in an activity or sport for pleasure rather than for money.

apartheid: A policy of keeping different races of people separated from one another.

balance beam: An elevated wooden beam several inches wide on which gymnasts perform athletic routines.

boycott: To refuse to engage in activities with a business, a group, or a nation to force it to change a plan or a policy.

breaststroke: A swimming stroke in which both arms are swept forward simultaneously and then drawn back with the palms outward, while the legs are at the same time drawn up and outward and then thrust back.

butterfly: A swimming stroke in which the extended arms are thrust up and over the shoulders and then down through the water, while the legs kick up and down.

decathlon: A track-and-field sport combining ten events: 100-meter, 400-meter, and 1500-meter races, 100-meter high hurdles, the javelin, the discus, shot put, pole vault, high jump, and broad jump.

diaulos: An ancient Greek Olympic race of two stadium lengths.

discus: A four-and-a-half-pound wood and metal disk that is thrown for distance in athletic events.

dolichos: An ancient Greek Olympic race of twenty-four stadium lengths.

eligibility: To have the required qualifications for a sports event.

federation: A union of various separate organizations.

fencing: A sports event involving thrusting and parrying with swords.

hippodrome: An oval stadium for horse and chariot races in ancient Greece.

hurdles: Barriers over which athletes leap during a race.

innovation: The discovery or introduction of a new idea or technique.

javelin: A slender shaft of wood and metal that is thrown for distance in a sports event.

marathon: A long-distance race of 26 miles, 385 yards.

nationalism: Having a prejudice in favor of one's own nation.

pancratium: An ancient Greek Olympic sport that combined wrestling, boxing, biting, kicking, gouging, or strangling.

parallel bars: A pair of bars of adjustable height and separation on which gymnasts perform athletic routines.

pentathlon: A track-and-field sport combining five events: the discus, the javelin, the long jump, and a 200-meter and a 1500-meter race.

professional: A person who engages in an activity or sport for pay.

propaganda: Spreading ideas and opinions to help or hurt a group or a nation.

quadrigae: An ancient Greek Olympic chariot race.

shot put: An athletic event in which a heavy metal ball is thrown for distance.

stade: A measurement of one stadium length.

steroid: A drug that increases the development of muscle tissue.

stimulant: A drug that increases speed and stamina.

vault: A gymnastic event in which athletes run and leap over a large, cushioned barrier.

velodrome: A stadium or auditorium containing a banked, oval track for bicycle races.

Suggestions for Further Reading

Matt Biondi, "Diary of a Champion," *Sports Illustrated*, October 3, 1988.

Lewis H. Carlson and John J. Fogarty, *Tales of Gold*. Chicago: Contemporary Books, 1987.

Allan Fotheringham, "Sportswriters' Big Drug Coverup," *MacLean's*, April 24, 1989.

Bruce Jenner and Marc Abraham, *Bruce Jenner's Guide to the Olympics*. Kansas City, MO: Andrews and McMeel, 1979.

John Kieran, Arthur Daley, and Pat Jordan, *The Story of the Olympic Games*. Philadelphia: J.B. Lippincott, 1977.

Bob Levin, "The Olympics: The Steroid Scandal," *MacLean's*, October 10, 1988.

Bill Mallon, Ian Buchanan, and Jeffrey Tishman, *Quest for Gold*. New York: Leisure Press, 1984.

Richard Manning, "The Selling of the Olympics," *Newsweek*, December 28, 1987.

Craig Neff, "Her Golden Moment," *Sports Illustrated*, September 26, 1988.

Dick Schaap, *An Illustrated History of the Olympics*. Third Edition, New York: Alfred A. Knopf, 1975.

Sports Illustrated, June 27, 1988, Special 1988 Winter Olympics Issue.

David Wallechinsky, *The Complete Book of the Olympics*. New York: Penguin Books, 1984.

Works Consulted

Ric Dolphin, "Sabotage at Seoul?" *MacLean's*, March 20, 1989.

Richard Espy, *The Politics of the Olympic Games.* Berkeley: University of California Press, 1979.

Juan Garcia, "Barcelona's Olympic Buildup," *World Press Review*, April 1989.

John V. Grombach, *The Olympics, 1960 Edition.* New York: Ballantine, 1960.

Allen Guttmann, *The Games Must Go On—Avery Brundage and the Olympic Movement.* New York: Columbia University Press, 1984.

William O. Johnson Jr., *All That Glitters Is Not Gold: An Irreverent Look at the Olympic Games.* New York: G.P. Putnam's Sons, 1972.

William O. Johnson Jr., "Gone with the Wind," *Sports Illustrated,* February 29, 1988.

William O. Johnson Jr., "Goodbye, Olive Wreaths, Hello, Riches and Reality," *Sports Illustrated,* February 9, 1987.

William O. Johnson Jr., "Is There Life After Los Angeles?" *Sports Illustrated*, May 21, 1984.

William O. Johnson Jr., "They Saved the Best for Last," *Sports Illustrated*, February 27, 1984.

John Lucas, *The Modern Olympic Games.* New York: A.S. Barnes, 1980.

John J. MacAloon, *This Great Symbol—Pierre de Coubertin and the Origins of the Modern Olympic Games.* Chicago: University of Chicago Press, 1981.

Richard D. Mandell, *The First Modern Olympics.* Berkeley: University of California Press, 1976.

Geoffrey Miller, *Behind the Olympic Rings.* Lynn, MA: H.O. Zimman, 1979.

Kenny Moore, "Oh, for the Days of a Country Fair," *Sports Illustrated*, May 21, 1984.

Kenny Moore, "They Got Off on the Right Track," *Sports Illustrated,* August 13, 1984.

Craig Neff, "Good and Tough," *Sports Illustrated*, October 3, 1988.

Craig Neff, "Swim Six, Win Six," *Sports Illustrated,* October 3, 1988.

Merrell Noden, "A Revealing Inquiry," *Sports Illustrated,* June 5, 1989.

Pat Putnam, "A Sad Day in Seoul," *Sports Illustrated,* October 3, 1988.

Pat Putnam, "Moses Moves Over," *Sports Illustrated,* October 3, 1988.

Kenneth Reich, "Doleful Days for the Games," *Sports Illustrated,* May 21, 1984.

Peter Stoler, "The Olympic Games That Companies Play," *Time*, February 22, 1988.

Harry Spencer Stuff, *The Story of the Olympic Games.* Los Angeles: Times-Mirror, 1931.

Robert Sullivan, "A Decline in the Gold Standard," *Sports Illustrated,* May 21, 1984.

E.M. Swift and Robert Sullivan, "An Olympic Quagmire," *Sports Illustrated,* March 7, 1988.

William Taaffe, "The $309 Million Games," *Sports Illustrated,* February 9, 1987.

Martin Barry Vinokur, *More Than A Game: Sports and Politics.* New York: Greenwood Press, 1988.

Barbara Wickens, "A Deepening Scandal," *MacLean's*, June 5, 1989.

Index

About the Author

Theodore Knight is a free-lance author and editor. He has also been a college professor and the manager of a large bookstore. Recently, Knight has worked on school textbooks in social studies, reading, and literature, and has edited books on art and on African culture, and writes a magazine book review column. Currently, Knight is writing a book about former president Jimmy Carter and a book about the winners of the Newbery and Caldecott awards for the best in children's books. Knight lives with his wife, son, and daughter in rural Rhode Island.

Picture Credits